A CHILD'S GUIDE TO ADVENT & CHRISTMAS

LOOK!

Laura Alary
Illustrated by Ann Boyajian

PARACLETE PRESS

BREWSTER, MASSACHUSETTS

2017 First Printing

Look! A Child's Guide to Advent and Christmas

Text Copyright © 2017 by Laura Alary
Illustrations Copyright © 2017 by Ann Boyajian

ISBN 978-1-61261-866-1

Library of Congress Cataloging-in-Publication Data
Names: Alary, Laura, author. | Boyajian, Ann, illustrator.
Title: Look! : a child's guide to Advent and Christmas / Laura Alary ;
   illustrated by Ann Boyajian.
Description: Brewster, Massachusetts : Paraclete Press, 2017.
Identifiers: LCCN 2017034862 | ISBN 9781612618661 (paperback)
Subjects: LCSH: Advent–Juvenile literature. | Christmas–Juvenile
   literature. | BISAC: RELIGION / Holidays / Christmas & Advent. | RELIGION
   / Christian Education / Children & Youth. | RELIGION / Christian Life /
   Family.
Classification: LCC BV40 .A44 2017 | DDC 263/.91–dc23
LC record available at https://lccn.loc.gov/2017034862

10 9 8 7 6 5 4 3 2 1

Published by Paraclete Press
Brewster, Massachusetts
www.paracletepress.com

Printed in the United States of America

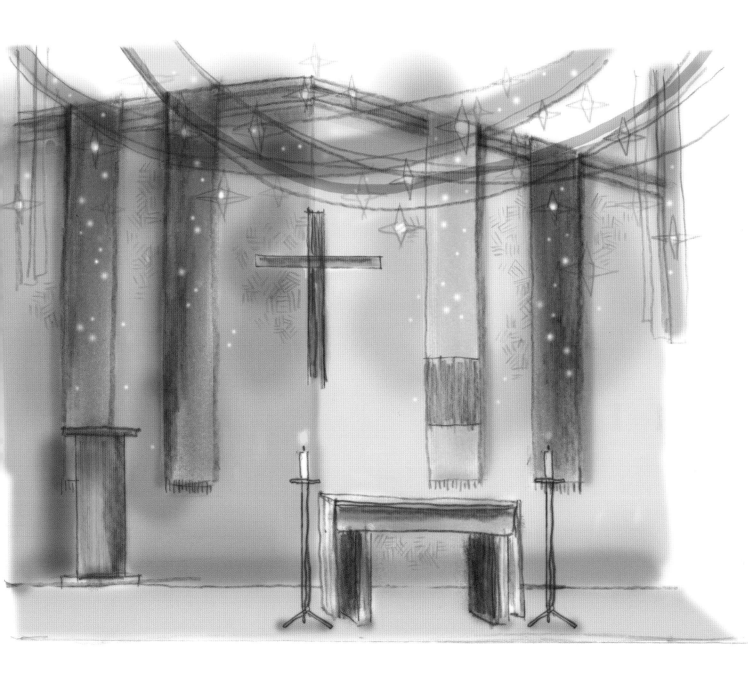

This is the season of Advent.
The church is dressed in purple.

The world outside has its own seasons and its own colors.
These days, the warm light of autumn is seeping away.
All the bright leaves have flown.
Winter is coming in black and white.
Furry frost coats the bare bones of trees,
and by suppertime we can already see the moon,
milky against the dark sky.

In a branch outside my window,
   squirrels have built a nest.
Even the shrubs are snug in their
   burlap blankets.
We are all huddled in the dark,
waiting for the light to return.

In church we are waiting too,
   waiting for Christmas.
While we wait,
   we watch for the light.

The People in Darkness

Long ago, the people of God huddled in the dark,

waiting and watching for the light.

It was a time of deep sadness.

Once they had lived happily in Jerusalem.

But an army destroyed their city,

their homes, their gardens, their holy places,

and carried the people far away across the desert.

Everything they knew and loved was gone.

All the color and light had seeped out of the world.

But in the darkness, God whispered messages of hope:

> *I will bring you home again.*

> *Where the ground is dry and cracked, a spring will bubble up.*

> *From a dead stump, bright green leaves will grow.*

> *On those who sit in deep darkness, light will shine.*

So even though they could not see the way ahead,
the people kept watching for the light.
I wonder if it was hard to hope?
Maybe they looked back and told stories
about how God had been with them in the past.
Maybe that helped them wait,
knowing they were not alone in the dark.

During Advent we look back.
We remember people who waited for God,
especially in times of trouble.
Every day we put a new ornament
   on our Jesse Tree.

Each one tells a story:

Noah and his family,
waiting for the storm to stop;

Abraham and Sarah,
waiting for a child;

The Hebrews in Egypt,
waiting to be free;

Miriam and Moses,
waiting to see the promised land;

The people of Jerusalem,
waiting to go home again.

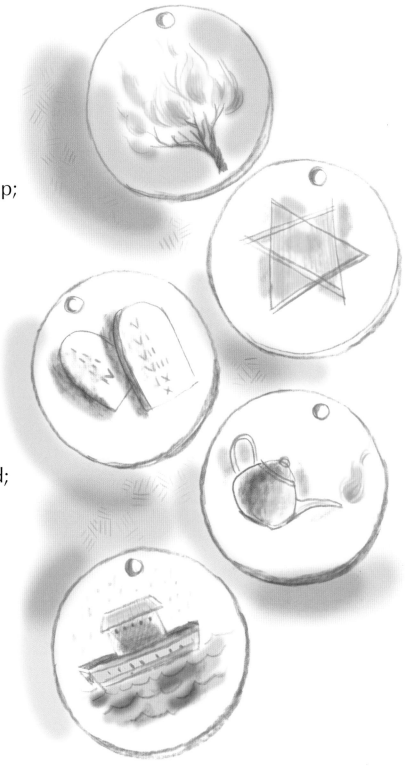

Sometimes I feel like I am waiting for something.
Sometimes I want God to come and help me.
Their stories are my story too.

During Advent we practice waiting and
   watching.
We look through old photo albums
and watch movies from when I was little.
We try to see how God was with us
in sad times and happy times.
Sometimes we see more clearly when we
   look back.
Every night we ask:
Where did I see God today?
Sometimes I write about it in my journal.
Sometimes I paint or draw.
Sometimes I use prayer beads.
          With each bead, I tell God what I hope for.

One night we bundle up and go outside to look at the stars.
We remember that God is in the darkness too.
Wherever I am, God is with me.

LOOK AROUND

John the Baptist

After many years, the people of God were still waiting.
They had come home to Jerusalem,
rebuilt their homes, gardens, and holy places,
but the world was still not the way they thought it should be.

So they began to hope for someone special,
someone who would come to set things right.
Who would it be? A wise king? A fierce soldier? A heavenly hero?
Someone to destroy their enemies
and rescue them from trouble?
No one knew for sure what God had in mind.

John the Baptist was waiting and watching
for whomever God might send.
When he was a young man,
John left his ordinary life
and went out into the desert.
When he came back,
he howled and stung like a sandstorm,
angry at the unfairness of the world:
 Someone is coming, he cried,
 Someone who will change everything!
 He will sort good from bad,
 the way a farmer separates wheat from chaff.
 And he will burn the chaff with fire.

Before this one comes, warned John, you must get ready:

 Change your ways!
 If you have two coats,
 Give one to someone who has none!
 Share your food with the hungry!
 Look around! See what needs to change!
 But change yourself first!

People who wanted to change came to John by the river.
Under the water they plunged, then up again—ready for a clean start.
One day Jesus came to be baptized.
When Jesus came up out of the dark water,
dazzled by brightness and fluttering wings,
John knew that Jesus was the one
he had been waiting for.

I wonder if Jesus was what John expected?
Jesus loved his enemies,
prayed for those who hurt him,
welcomed everyone—good and bad together.
Sometimes God comes in ways we don't expect.
Maybe God likes surprises.

During Advent we look around.

We try to see the things we usually miss.

We read stories about people in other places

and imagine what their lives are like.

Some of the stories are sad.

Why do some people have so much,

and others not enough?

The world is still not the way it should be.

The stories push us to ask hard questions:

  What needs to change?

  Is there anything we say or do that hurts others,

  near or far away?

  How can we change our ways?

At supper we say a new kind of prayer.
Before we eat, we try to think of everyone
who helped bring the food to our table.

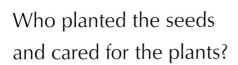

Who planted the seeds
and cared for the plants?

Who picked the fruit
and dug the vegetables?

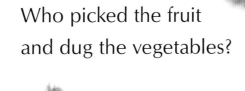

Who brought them to market?

We thank God for everyone.
We are all connected.

During Advent we share.
We collect food and toys,
coats and boots,
for people who have none.

One day we make special wreaths.

On green paper, we trace our hands many times,

then cut out the shapes and put them in a basket.

Whenever we do something kind,

we glue another hand to the wreath.

Day by day, the wreath gets fuller.

It feels good to see how we are helping.

But the wreath helps us too.

It reminds us to look around

and see how we can make the world better.

Advent is a time for surprises.
Each door of our calendar
hides a tiny gift—one for every day.
Even better are the surprises we create.
With paints and potato stamps
we make Advent cards.
On each one we write a hopeful message
to someone who needs cheer.
We hope the cards will be a bright spot in
   a dull day.

One afternoon we bake cookies
and pack them in pretty boxes.
That night we load the boxes into our
   wagon
and walk around the block,
delivering treats to our neighbors.

20

Their faces say more than words:
Wonder. Thanks. Joy. Delight.
On the walk home, the wagon is empty,
but my heart is full.
Sometimes I think I can see God in other people.
I wonder if they can see God in me?
God comes in ways we don't expect.

Mary

Mary was waiting too,
counting the days until her wedding.
While she waited, she dreamed—
dreamed of a new life with Joseph,
of the children she hoped to have,
maybe even grandchildren someday.
But into her daydreams burst the messenger
with his astonishing words:

> Greetings, Mary.
> The blessing of God is upon you.
> The Holy Spirit will overshadow you,
> and you will have a child,
> who will be called the Son of the Most High God,
> a light for people everywhere.

Mary wondered:
How can this be?
I am not even married yet!
What will people say?
What will Joseph say?
Will he believe me?
What will this child become?
How can he possibly be
the One we have all been waiting for?

I wonder if Mary could have said no?
What would have happened then?
Maybe God would have found some other way.
Then Mary would have lost her chance
to bring God into the world.
But Mary said yes,
Sang yes, her voice trembling with fear and joy.

During Advent, we look ahead.
We think about our own choices.

What is God asking us to do and be?
I often say no:

    No, I don't want to.
    No, I'm busy.
    No, I'm too scared.

I wonder if I have ever said no to God?
I wonder what might have happened if I had said *yes*?

Each Sunday of Advent
we light a new candle on the Advent wreath.
I love how the light grows and grows.
Three of the candles are purple.
But on the third Sunday,
the candle is pink.

People say that is because pink is the color of joy.
We are joyful because it is almost Christmas.
Our waiting is almost over.
But I like to think there is another reason.
Pink is the color of new things:
sunrise, baby birds, cherry blossoms in the spring.
When I draw a picture of Mary, I dress her in pink,
not the usual blue.
Mary said yes to something new.
And her yes brought the light of God into the world.
That makes me joyful.

During Advent, we try to be brave like Mary
and say yes to new things.
We ask a new family to come for lunch.
I talk to the girl who has just moved to my school.
We peel potatoes at the soup kitchen
and visit with the people who have come for a hot meal.
Maybe we have made the world a little brighter.

I can see how *no* slams the door,
but *yes* lets God come in.

Christmas

One night in Bethlehem,
months of waiting came to an end.
It was not what Mary had expected.
She had imagined giving birth at home,
within the warm, safe circle of her family.
But the baby came in his own surprising way.
Cuddling him by lamplight,
Mary marveled over his tiny fingers and toes.

How could someone so small
fill her with so much love?

Soon, others came looking for the child:
shepherds, with their bleating sheep,
following rumors of a savior;
women from the village, with steaming dishes of food,
drawn by compassion and curiosity;
scholars, with books and star charts and precious gifts,
thirsty for truth and wisdom;
a bitter, fearful king,
bent on destroying what he could not understand;
and later, old Simeon and Anna,
who came to the Temple day after day,
patiently waiting for the one who would save their people.
Each one came looking for something.

Except Mary.

For her it was enough simply to be with Jesus.

Very late on Christmas Eve
we go to church.
The sanctuary is still dark,
except for the Advent wreath.
All four candles are burning.
Their flames dance in the shadows.
Only the tall, white Christ candle remains to be lit.

We listen to words from the Bible,
ancient words from people who
wondered, watched,
and waited for God to come.

Then something wonderful happens.
With the flare of a match,
the Christ candle leaps to life.
Someone touches its flame with a taper,
and passes on the light.
Each of us holds a small candle.
One by one, we receive the light,
and pass it on.
The Christ light grows and grows
until all our faces are glowing.
I can feel the Mystery.

I used to wonder how we could still be waiting

for someone born so long ago.

But now I see.

In Jesus, the light of the world,

God came to us in a new and surprising way.

But not for the first time.

And not for the last.

Whenever we say yes to God,

the light of Christ shines through us

in a new place and time.

Advent helps us see and remember

what is always true:

In the darkness or in the light,

God is with us.

Advent is over now.

We have looked back.

We have looked around.

We have looked ahead.

We are ready now.

The light shines in the darkness.

God is here.

It is Christmas morning.